50 Classic BBQ Sides and Mains

By: Kelly Johnson

Table of Contents

- Grilled Corn on the Cob
- Classic Coleslaw
- Potato Salad
- Baked Beans
- Grilled Asparagus
- Macaroni and Cheese
- Grilled Vegetable Skewers
- Cornbread
- Caesar Salad
- Grilled Chicken Wings
- Pulled Pork Sandwiches
- BBQ Ribs
- Grilled Sausages
- Coleslaw with Apple and Carrot
- Roasted Garlic Mashed Potatoes
- Grilled Shrimp Skewers
- Sweet Potato Fries
- Jalapeño Cornbread
- Grilled Portobello Mushrooms
- Charred Brussels Sprouts
- Bacon-Wrapped Hot Dogs
- Grilled Pineapple
- Fried Pickles
- Grilled Salmon
- BBQ Chicken Thighs
- Caprese Salad
- Grilled Steak
- Grilled Zucchini
- Spicy Pickled Onions
- Grilled Flatbreads
- Buffalo Cauliflower Bites
- Chickpea Salad
- Avocado and Tomato Salad
- Grilled Peppers and Onions
- Garlic Bread

- Smoked Brisket
- Roasted Beet Salad
- Grilled Eggplant
- Pimento Cheese Dip
- Macaroni Salad with Bacon
- Southern Biscuits
- Grilled Tuna Steaks
- Cucumber Salad
- BBQ Pork Sliders
- Grilled Lobster Tails
- Smoked Sausages
- Corn and Tomato Salad
- Grilled Clams
- Cilantro Lime Rice
- BBQ Pulled Chicken

Grilled Corn on the Cob

Ingredients

- 4 ears of corn, husked
- 2 tablespoons butter (optional)
- Salt and pepper to taste
- Fresh herbs like parsley or cilantro (optional)

Instructions

1. Preheat the grill to medium heat.
2. Place the corn on the grill and cook, turning every 2-3 minutes, for about 10-15 minutes, or until the kernels are tender and lightly charred.
3. Brush with butter, sprinkle with salt, pepper, and fresh herbs, if desired.
4. Serve warm.

Classic Coleslaw

Ingredients

- 4 cups shredded cabbage
- 1 cup shredded carrots
- 1/2 cup mayonnaise
- 2 tablespoons apple cider vinegar
- 1 tablespoon sugar
- 1 teaspoon mustard (optional)
- Salt and pepper to taste

Instructions

1. In a large bowl, combine cabbage and carrots.
2. In a small bowl, whisk together mayonnaise, vinegar, sugar, mustard, salt, and pepper.
3. Pour the dressing over the cabbage mixture and toss to coat evenly.
4. Chill in the refrigerator for at least 1 hour before serving.

Potato Salad

Ingredients

- 4 cups boiled and cubed potatoes
- 1/2 cup mayonnaise
- 2 tablespoons Dijon mustard
- 2 tablespoons apple cider vinegar
- 1/2 cup chopped celery
- 1/4 cup chopped red onion
- Salt and pepper to taste

Instructions

1. In a large bowl, mix together the boiled potatoes, celery, and onion.
2. In a separate bowl, whisk together the mayonnaise, mustard, and vinegar.
3. Pour the dressing over the potato mixture and stir to combine.
4. Season with salt and pepper and refrigerate for 2-3 hours before serving.

Baked Beans

Ingredients

- 2 cans (15 oz each) baked beans
- 1/4 cup brown sugar
- 1/4 cup ketchup
- 1 tablespoon mustard
- 1/2 cup diced bacon (optional)
- 1/2 onion, finely chopped

Instructions

1. Preheat the oven to 350°F (175°C).
2. In a saucepan, cook the bacon until crispy, then remove and chop into pieces.
3. In a mixing bowl, combine the baked beans, brown sugar, ketchup, mustard, and bacon.
4. Pour the mixture into a baking dish and bake for 30-40 minutes, or until bubbly and caramelized.
5. Serve warm.

Grilled Asparagus

Ingredients

- 1 bunch asparagus, trimmed
- 2 tablespoons olive oil
- Salt and pepper to taste
- Lemon wedges for serving

Instructions

1. Preheat the grill to medium heat.
2. Toss the asparagus with olive oil, salt, and pepper.
3. Grill the asparagus for 5-7 minutes, turning occasionally, until tender and lightly charred.
4. Serve with lemon wedges.

Macaroni and Cheese

Ingredients

- 2 cups elbow macaroni
- 2 cups shredded cheddar cheese
- 1 cup milk
- 2 tablespoons butter
- 2 tablespoons all-purpose flour
- Salt and pepper to taste

Instructions

1. Cook the macaroni according to package instructions and drain.
2. In a saucepan, melt butter and whisk in flour until smooth.
3. Gradually add the milk, stirring constantly until the sauce thickens.
4. Stir in the cheese until melted and smooth.
5. Combine the cooked macaroni with the cheese sauce and season with salt and pepper.
6. Serve warm.

Grilled Vegetable Skewers

Ingredients

- 1 zucchini, sliced
- 1 bell pepper, cut into chunks
- 1 red onion, cut into chunks
- 1 cup cherry tomatoes
- 2 tablespoons olive oil
- 1 teaspoon dried oregano
- Salt and pepper to taste

Instructions

1. Preheat the grill to medium heat.
2. Thread the vegetables onto skewers, alternating the pieces.
3. Brush with olive oil and season with oregano, salt, and pepper.
4. Grill the skewers for 5-7 minutes, turning occasionally, until the vegetables are tender and lightly charred.
5. Serve immediately.

Cornbread

Ingredients

- 1 cup cornmeal
- 1 cup all-purpose flour
- 1/4 cup sugar
- 1 tablespoon baking powder
- 1/2 teaspoon salt
- 1 cup milk
- 2 eggs
- 1/4 cup melted butter

Instructions

1. Preheat the oven to 375°F (190°C) and grease a baking pan.
2. In a bowl, combine cornmeal, flour, sugar, baking powder, and salt.
3. In another bowl, whisk together milk, eggs, and melted butter.
4. Add the wet ingredients to the dry ingredients and stir until just combined.
5. Pour the batter into the prepared pan and bake for 25-30 minutes, or until a toothpick comes out clean.
6. Serve warm.

Caesar Salad

Ingredients

- 6 cups romaine lettuce, chopped
- 1/2 cup Caesar dressing
- 1/4 cup grated Parmesan cheese
- 1/4 cup croutons

Instructions

1. In a large bowl, toss the lettuce with Caesar dressing.
2. Sprinkle with Parmesan cheese and top with croutons.
3. Serve immediately.

Grilled Chicken Wings

Ingredients

- 10 chicken wings
- 2 tablespoons olive oil
- 1 tablespoon paprika
- 1 teaspoon garlic powder
- 1 teaspoon onion powder
- Salt and pepper to taste

Instructions

1. Preheat the grill to medium heat.
2. Toss the chicken wings in olive oil, paprika, garlic powder, onion powder, salt, and pepper.
3. Grill the wings for 15-20 minutes, turning occasionally, until they are golden brown and cooked through.
4. Serve hot.

Pulled Pork Sandwiches

Ingredients

- 2 pounds pork shoulder
- 1 cup barbecue sauce
- 1 tablespoon apple cider vinegar
- 1 tablespoon brown sugar
- 4 hamburger buns

Instructions

1. Preheat the oven to 300°F (150°C).
2. Rub the pork shoulder with salt and pepper, then place it in a roasting pan.
3. Roast for 3-4 hours, or until the pork is tender and easily shredded.
4. Shred the pork and mix it with barbecue sauce, apple cider vinegar, and brown sugar.
5. Serve the pulled pork on hamburger buns with extra barbecue sauce if desired.

BBQ Ribs

Ingredients

- 2 racks of baby back ribs
- 1/4 cup brown sugar
- 2 tablespoons paprika
- 1 tablespoon chili powder
- 1 tablespoon garlic powder
- 1 teaspoon onion powder
- Salt and pepper to taste
- 1 cup BBQ sauce

Instructions

1. Preheat the grill to medium-low heat.
2. In a small bowl, combine brown sugar, paprika, chili powder, garlic powder, onion powder, salt, and pepper.
3. Rub the spice mixture evenly on both sides of the ribs.
4. Place the ribs on the grill, bone-side down, and cook for 2-3 hours, turning occasionally, until tender.
5. During the last 30 minutes, brush the ribs with BBQ sauce and cook until the sauce caramelizes.
6. Serve with extra BBQ sauce on the side.

Grilled Sausages

Ingredients

- 6 sausages (your choice of flavor)
- 1 tablespoon olive oil
- Salt and pepper to taste

Instructions

1. Preheat the grill to medium heat.
2. Brush the sausages with olive oil and season with salt and pepper.
3. Grill the sausages for 10-12 minutes, turning occasionally, until they are cooked through and browned.
4. Serve with your favorite condiments and sides.

Coleslaw with Apple and Carrot

Ingredients

- 4 cups shredded cabbage
- 1 apple, thinly sliced
- 1 carrot, grated
- 1/2 cup mayonnaise
- 1 tablespoon apple cider vinegar
- 1 tablespoon honey
- Salt and pepper to taste

Instructions

1. In a large bowl, combine cabbage, apple, and carrot.
2. In a separate bowl, whisk together mayonnaise, vinegar, honey, salt, and pepper.
3. Pour the dressing over the cabbage mixture and toss to combine.
4. Refrigerate for 30 minutes before serving.

Roasted Garlic Mashed Potatoes

Ingredients

- 4 large potatoes, peeled and cubed
- 4 cloves garlic, minced
- 1/2 cup heavy cream
- 1/4 cup butter
- Salt and pepper to taste

Instructions

1. Boil the potatoes in salted water until tender, about 15 minutes.
2. While the potatoes cook, sauté garlic in butter over medium heat until fragrant.
3. Drain the potatoes and mash them with the garlic butter, heavy cream, salt, and pepper.
4. Serve warm.

Grilled Shrimp Skewers

Ingredients

- 1 pound large shrimp, peeled and deveined
- 2 tablespoons olive oil
- 1 tablespoon lemon juice
- 2 garlic cloves, minced
- 1 teaspoon paprika
- Salt and pepper to taste

Instructions

1. Preheat the grill to medium-high heat.
2. In a bowl, combine olive oil, lemon juice, garlic, paprika, salt, and pepper.
3. Toss the shrimp in the marinade and thread them onto skewers.
4. Grill the shrimp for 2-3 minutes per side, until pink and opaque.
5. Serve with lemon wedges.

Sweet Potato Fries

Ingredients

- 2 large sweet potatoes, peeled and cut into fries
- 2 tablespoons olive oil
- 1 teaspoon paprika
- 1/2 teaspoon garlic powder
- Salt and pepper to taste

Instructions

1. Preheat the oven to 425°F (220°C).
2. Toss the sweet potato fries with olive oil, paprika, garlic powder, salt, and pepper.
3. Arrange the fries in a single layer on a baking sheet.
4. Roast for 20-25 minutes, flipping halfway through, until crispy and golden.
5. Serve hot.

Jalapeño Cornbread

Ingredients

- 1 cup cornmeal
- 1 cup all-purpose flour
- 1/4 cup sugar
- 1 tablespoon baking powder
- 1/2 teaspoon salt
- 1/2 cup milk
- 2 eggs
- 1/4 cup melted butter
- 1/2 cup chopped jalapeños (seeds removed)

Instructions

1. Preheat the oven to 375°F (190°C) and grease a baking dish.
2. In a bowl, combine cornmeal, flour, sugar, baking powder, and salt.
3. In another bowl, whisk together milk, eggs, and melted butter.
4. Add the wet ingredients to the dry ingredients, then fold in the jalapeños.
5. Pour the batter into the prepared dish and bake for 25-30 minutes, or until a toothpick comes out clean.
6. Serve warm.

Grilled Portobello Mushrooms

Ingredients

- 4 large Portobello mushroom caps
- 2 tablespoons olive oil
- 1 tablespoon balsamic vinegar
- 2 cloves garlic, minced
- Salt and pepper to taste

Instructions

1. Preheat the grill to medium heat.
2. In a bowl, mix olive oil, balsamic vinegar, garlic, salt, and pepper.
3. Brush the mushroom caps with the mixture and place them on the grill.
4. Grill for 5-7 minutes per side, until tender and slightly charred.
5. Serve as a side dish or on a bun for a vegetarian burger.

Charred Brussels Sprouts

Ingredients

- 1 pound Brussels sprouts, halved
- 2 tablespoons olive oil
- Salt and pepper to taste

Instructions

1. Preheat the grill to medium-high heat.
2. Toss Brussels sprouts with olive oil, salt, and pepper.
3. Place them on the grill, cut-side down, and cook for 6-8 minutes, flipping halfway through, until charred and tender.
4. Serve immediately.

Bacon-Wrapped Hot Dogs

Ingredients

- 4 hot dogs
- 4 slices of bacon
- 1 tablespoon olive oil

Instructions

1. Preheat the grill to medium heat.
2. Wrap each hot dog with a slice of bacon and secure with toothpicks.
3. Brush with olive oil and grill for 7-10 minutes, turning occasionally, until the bacon is crispy.
4. Serve on buns with your favorite toppings.

Grilled Pineapple

Ingredients

- 1 fresh pineapple, peeled, cored, and sliced into rings
- 2 tablespoons honey
- 1/2 teaspoon ground cinnamon

Instructions

1. Preheat the grill to medium heat.
2. Brush the pineapple rings with honey and sprinkle with cinnamon.
3. Grill the pineapple for 2-3 minutes per side, until caramelized and grill marks appear.
4. Serve as a side dish or dessert.

Fried Pickles

Ingredients

- 1 jar dill pickles, sliced
- 1 cup all-purpose flour
- 1 teaspoon paprika
- 1 teaspoon garlic powder
- 1/2 teaspoon cayenne pepper
- 1/2 teaspoon salt
- 1/4 teaspoon black pepper
- 1 egg, beaten
- 1/2 cup buttermilk
- Vegetable oil, for frying

Instructions

1. In a shallow bowl, whisk together flour, paprika, garlic powder, cayenne, salt, and pepper.
2. In another bowl, combine the egg and buttermilk.
3. Dip pickle slices into the egg mixture, then coat in the seasoned flour.
4. Heat oil in a deep pan over medium-high heat.
5. Fry the pickles in batches for 2-3 minutes or until golden and crispy.
6. Drain on paper towels and serve with ranch dressing.

Grilled Salmon

Ingredients

- 4 salmon fillets
- 2 tablespoons olive oil
- 1 tablespoon lemon juice
- 1 teaspoon garlic powder
- Salt and pepper to taste
- Lemon wedges for garnish

Instructions

1. Preheat the grill to medium-high heat.
2. Brush salmon fillets with olive oil and lemon juice. Season with garlic powder, salt, and pepper.
3. Grill the salmon for 4-5 minutes per side, or until it flakes easily with a fork.
4. Serve with lemon wedges.

BBQ Chicken Thighs

Ingredients

- 8 bone-in, skin-on chicken thighs
- 1/4 cup BBQ sauce
- Salt and pepper to taste

Instructions

1. Preheat the grill to medium-high heat.
2. Season the chicken thighs with salt and pepper.
3. Grill the chicken for 6-7 minutes per side, basting with BBQ sauce halfway through.
4. Cook until the internal temperature reaches 165°F (75°C).
5. Serve with additional BBQ sauce on the side.

Caprese Salad

Ingredients

- 3 large tomatoes, sliced
- 8 oz fresh mozzarella, sliced
- 1/4 cup fresh basil leaves
- 2 tablespoons balsamic glaze
- 1 tablespoon olive oil
- Salt and pepper to taste

Instructions

1. Arrange the tomato and mozzarella slices on a plate.
2. Sprinkle with fresh basil leaves.
3. Drizzle with balsamic glaze and olive oil.
4. Season with salt and pepper.
5. Serve chilled or at room temperature.

Grilled Steak

Ingredients

- 2 ribeye or sirloin steaks
- 1 tablespoon olive oil
- Salt and pepper to taste
- 2 cloves garlic, minced
- 2 tablespoons fresh rosemary, chopped

Instructions

1. Preheat the grill to high heat.
2. Brush the steaks with olive oil and season with salt, pepper, garlic, and rosemary.
3. Grill steaks for 4-5 minutes per side for medium-rare, or adjust to your desired doneness.
4. Let the steaks rest for 5 minutes before serving

Grilled Zucchini

Ingredients

- 2 zucchinis, sliced into thick rounds
- 2 tablespoons olive oil
- Salt and pepper to taste
- 1/2 teaspoon dried oregano

Instructions

1. Preheat the grill to medium heat.
2. Toss the zucchini slices with olive oil, salt, pepper, and oregano.
3. Grill the zucchini for 3-4 minutes per side, until tender and lightly charred.
4. Serve as a side dish or on top of a salad.

Spicy Pickled Onions

Ingredients

- 1 large red onion, thinly sliced
- 1 cup vinegar (white or apple cider)
- 1/4 cup sugar
- 1 tablespoon salt
- 1-2 teaspoons red pepper flakes
- 1 cup water

Instructions

1. In a saucepan, combine vinegar, sugar, salt, red pepper flakes, and water. Bring to a simmer over medium heat, stirring until the sugar dissolves.
2. Place the onion slices in a jar or bowl.
3. Pour the hot vinegar mixture over the onions, making sure they're fully submerged.
4. Let sit for at least 30 minutes, or refrigerate for up to a week.

Grilled Flatbreads

Ingredients

- 2 cups all-purpose flour
- 1 teaspoon baking powder
- 1/2 teaspoon salt
- 3/4 cup warm water
- 1 tablespoon olive oil
- 1 teaspoon garlic powder

Instructions

1. In a large bowl, combine flour, baking powder, and salt.
2. Gradually add warm water, stirring to form a dough.
3. Knead the dough on a floured surface until smooth.
4. Divide the dough into small balls and roll out into flat rounds.
5. Heat a grill or grill pan over medium-high heat.
6. Grill the flatbreads for 2-3 minutes per side, until lightly charred.
7. Brush with olive oil and garlic powder before serving.

Buffalo Cauliflower Bites

Ingredients

- 1 medium cauliflower, cut into florets
- 1/2 cup flour
- 1/2 cup water
- 1 teaspoon garlic powder
- 1/2 teaspoon paprika
- Salt and pepper to taste
- 1/2 cup buffalo sauce
- 1 tablespoon olive oil

Instructions

1. Preheat the oven to 400°F (200°C).
2. In a bowl, whisk together flour, water, garlic powder, paprika, salt, and pepper.
3. Dip each cauliflower floret into the batter, then place on a baking sheet.
4. Bake for 20 minutes, flipping halfway through.
5. Toss the cauliflower in buffalo sauce and bake for an additional 5-10 minutes.
6. Serve with ranch or blue cheese dressing.

Chickpea Salad

Ingredients

- 1 can (15 oz) chickpeas, drained and rinsed
- 1 cucumber, diced
- 1 red bell pepper, diced
- 1/4 cup red onion, finely chopped
- 1/4 cup fresh parsley, chopped
- 2 tablespoons olive oil
- 1 tablespoon lemon juice
- Salt and pepper to taste

Instructions

1. In a large bowl, combine chickpeas, cucumber, bell pepper, onion, and parsley.
2. Drizzle with olive oil and lemon juice, and toss to combine.
3. Season with salt and pepper to taste.
4. Serve chilled or at room temperature.

Avocado and Tomato Salad

Ingredients

- 2 ripe avocados, diced
- 2 large tomatoes, diced
- 1 small red onion, finely chopped
- 1/4 cup fresh cilantro, chopped
- 1 tablespoon olive oil
- 1 tablespoon lime juice
- Salt and pepper to taste

Instructions

1. In a bowl, combine the diced avocados, tomatoes, and red onion.
2. Drizzle with olive oil and lime juice.
3. Toss gently to combine.
4. Season with salt, pepper, and cilantro.
5. Serve chilled.

Grilled Peppers and Onions

Ingredients

- 2 bell peppers, sliced
- 1 red onion, sliced
- 2 tablespoons olive oil
- 1 teaspoon balsamic vinegar
- Salt and pepper to taste

Instructions

1. Preheat the grill to medium-high heat.
2. Toss the peppers and onions in olive oil, balsamic vinegar, salt, and pepper.
3. Grill the vegetables for 5-7 minutes, turning occasionally, until tender and lightly charred.
4. Serve immediately as a side dish or topping for burgers.

Garlic Bread

Ingredients

- 1 loaf Italian bread or baguette
- 1/2 cup butter, softened
- 4 cloves garlic, minced
- 2 tablespoons fresh parsley, chopped
- Salt to taste

Instructions

1. Preheat the oven to 375°F (190°C).
2. Slice the bread into thick pieces.
3. In a bowl, combine the softened butter, minced garlic, parsley, and salt.
4. Spread the garlic butter mixture generously on each slice of bread.
5. Bake for 10-12 minutes, or until golden and crispy.
6. Serve warm.

Smoked Brisket

Ingredients

- 1 whole beef brisket (5-6 lbs)
- 2 tablespoons olive oil
- 1/4 cup beef rub (or a mix of salt, pepper, garlic powder, and paprika)
- Wood chips (oak or hickory)

Instructions

1. Preheat your smoker to 225°F (107°C).
2. Rub the brisket with olive oil and season generously with the beef rub.
3. Place the brisket in the smoker and cook for 10-12 hours, or until the internal temperature reaches 195°F (90°C).
4. Let the brisket rest for 30 minutes before slicing and serving.

Roasted Beet Salad

Ingredients

- 4 medium beets, peeled and cubed
- 2 tablespoons olive oil
- Salt and pepper to taste
- 1/4 cup goat cheese, crumbled
- 1/4 cup walnuts, toasted
- 2 tablespoons balsamic vinegar

Instructions

1. Preheat the oven to 400°F (200°C).
2. Toss the cubed beets in olive oil, salt, and pepper.
3. Roast on a baking sheet for 30-40 minutes, turning once, until tender.
4. Let the beets cool slightly.
5. Toss with goat cheese, walnuts, and balsamic vinegar.
6. Serve chilled or at room temperature.

Grilled Eggplant

Ingredients

- 2 medium eggplants, sliced into rounds
- 3 tablespoons olive oil
- 1 tablespoon balsamic vinegar
- 2 cloves garlic, minced
- Salt and pepper to taste

Instructions

1. Preheat the grill to medium heat.
2. Brush the eggplant slices with olive oil and balsamic vinegar.
3. Sprinkle with minced garlic, salt, and pepper.
4. Grill the eggplant for 3-4 minutes per side, until tender and lightly charred.
5. Serve immediately as a side dish or topping for sandwiches.

Pimento Cheese Dip

Ingredients

- 8 oz cream cheese, softened
- 1/2 cup mayonnaise
- 1 1/2 cups shredded cheddar cheese
- 1/2 cup pimentos, drained and chopped
- 1/2 teaspoon garlic powder
- Salt and pepper to taste

Instructions

1. In a bowl, combine the cream cheese and mayonnaise.
2. Stir in the shredded cheddar cheese, pimentos, garlic powder, salt, and pepper.
3. Mix until smooth and well combined.
4. Serve with crackers or veggies for dipping.

Macaroni Salad with Bacon

Ingredients

- 2 cups elbow macaroni, cooked and drained
- 1/2 cup mayonnaise
- 1 tablespoon Dijon mustard
- 2 tablespoons white vinegar
- 1/4 cup red onion, finely chopped
- 1/4 cup celery, diced
- 1/2 cup cooked bacon, crumbled
- Salt and pepper to taste

Instructions

1. In a large bowl, combine the cooked macaroni, mayonnaise, Dijon mustard, and vinegar.
2. Add the red onion, celery, bacon, salt, and pepper.
3. Stir until well combined.
4. Chill for at least 1 hour before serving.

Southern Biscuits

Ingredients

- 2 cups all-purpose flour
- 2 teaspoons baking powder
- 1/2 teaspoon salt
- 1/2 cup cold butter, cubed
- 3/4 cup milk

Instructions

1. Preheat the oven to 450°F (230°C).
2. In a bowl, combine the flour, baking powder, and salt.
3. Cut in the cold butter using a pastry cutter until the mixture resembles coarse crumbs.
4. Stir in the milk until just combined.
5. Turn the dough out onto a floured surface and gently knead.
6. Roll out to 1/2 inch thick, then cut into rounds.
7. Place the biscuits on a baking sheet and bake for 10-12 minutes, or until golden brown.
8. Serve warm.

Grilled Tuna Steaks

Ingredients

- 4 tuna steaks
- 2 tablespoons olive oil
- 1 tablespoon soy sauce
- 1 tablespoon lemon juice
- Salt and pepper to taste

Instructions

1. Preheat the grill to medium-high heat.
2. Brush the tuna steaks with olive oil, soy sauce, lemon juice, salt, and pepper.
3. Grill the steaks for 2-3 minutes per side, depending on thickness and desired doneness.
4. Serve immediately with a squeeze of lemon.

Cucumber Salad

Ingredients

- 2 cucumbers, thinly sliced
- 1/2 red onion, thinly sliced
- 1/4 cup fresh dill, chopped
- 1/4 cup white vinegar
- 1 tablespoon olive oil
- 1 teaspoon sugar
- Salt and pepper to taste

Instructions

1. In a large bowl, combine the sliced cucumbers, red onion, and dill.
2. In a small bowl, whisk together the vinegar, olive oil, sugar, salt, and pepper.
3. Pour the dressing over the cucumbers and toss to combine.
4. Let sit in the fridge for at least 30 minutes before serving for the flavors to meld.

BBQ Pork Sliders

Ingredients

- 1 lb pulled pork (cooked and shredded)
- 1/2 cup BBQ sauce
- 12 slider buns
- 1/4 cup coleslaw (optional)

Instructions

1. In a pan, heat the pulled pork and BBQ sauce over medium heat until warmed through.
2. Toast the slider buns lightly on a grill or skillet.
3. Assemble the sliders by placing a generous scoop of BBQ pork on the bottom half of each bun.
4. Top with coleslaw, if desired, and cover with the top half of the bun.
5. Serve immediately with extra BBQ sauce on the side.

Grilled Lobster Tails

Ingredients

- 4 lobster tails
- 2 tablespoons melted butter
- 2 cloves garlic, minced
- 1 tablespoon lemon juice
- Salt and pepper to taste
- Fresh parsley for garnish

Instructions

1. Preheat the grill to medium-high heat.
2. Using kitchen scissors, cut the lobster tails in half lengthwise, leaving the shell intact.
3. In a small bowl, mix together the melted butter, garlic, lemon juice, salt, and pepper.
4. Brush the lobster meat with the butter mixture.
5. Grill the lobster tails meat-side down for 4-5 minutes, then flip and grill for an additional 2-3 minutes, until the lobster is opaque.
6. Garnish with fresh parsley and serve with lemon wedges.

Smoked Sausages

Ingredients

- 6 smoked sausages (your choice of flavor)
- 1 tablespoon olive oil
- 1/4 cup yellow mustard (optional)

Instructions

1. Preheat the grill to medium heat.
2. Lightly oil the grill grates or brush the sausages with olive oil.
3. Grill the sausages for 6-8 minutes, turning occasionally, until browned and heated through.
4. Serve with mustard or your favorite condiments.

Corn and Tomato Salad

Ingredients

- 2 cups cooked corn kernels (fresh or frozen)
- 2 cups cherry tomatoes, halved
- 1/4 cup red onion, finely chopped
- 1/4 cup fresh cilantro, chopped
- 2 tablespoons olive oil
- 1 tablespoon lime juice
- Salt and pepper to taste

Instructions

1. In a bowl, combine the corn, tomatoes, red onion, and cilantro.
2. Drizzle with olive oil and lime juice.
3. Toss gently to combine and season with salt and pepper.
4. Serve chilled or at room temperature.

Grilled Clams

Ingredients

- 2 dozen fresh clams
- 2 tablespoons melted butter
- 2 cloves garlic, minced
- 1 tablespoon fresh parsley, chopped
- Lemon wedges for serving

Instructions

1. Preheat the grill to medium-high heat.
2. Scrub the clams and place them on the grill.
3. Grill for 5-7 minutes, or until the clams open up.
4. While the clams are grilling, combine the melted butter, garlic, and parsley in a small bowl.
5. Once the clams open, brush with the garlic butter mixture and serve immediately with lemon wedges.

Cilantro Lime Rice

Ingredients

- 1 cup basmati rice
- 2 cups water
- 1 tablespoon olive oil
- Juice of 1 lime
- 1/4 cup fresh cilantro, chopped
- Salt to taste

Instructions

1. In a saucepan, bring the water to a boil.
2. Add the rice, olive oil, and salt. Reduce the heat to low, cover, and cook for 15-20 minutes, or until the rice is tender and the water has been absorbed.
3. Fluff the rice with a fork and stir in the lime juice and cilantro.
4. Serve warm.

BBQ Pulled Chicken

Ingredients

- 1 lb cooked chicken breasts (shredded)
- 1/2 cup BBQ sauce
- 12 slider buns
- 1/4 cup coleslaw (optional)

Instructions

1. In a pan, heat the shredded chicken and BBQ sauce over medium heat until warmed through.
2. Toast the slider buns lightly.
3. Assemble the pulled chicken sandwiches by placing a generous amount of BBQ chicken on each bun.
4. Top with coleslaw, if desired, and close with the top bun.
5. Serve immediately with extra BBQ sauce on the side.

www.ingramcontent.com/pod-product-compliance
Lightning Source LLC
LaVergne TN
LVHW081333060526
838201LV00055B/2620